CW01593990

Author's Note

Bisexuality is not simply a case of liking a bit of both, just as bipolarism is far more complex than episodes of pure mania and stark depression. Love is not the uncomplicated solution to abuse… but it certainly helps the recovery.

This book is all about the extremes, the far reaches and the fringes. I hope it hits you in stereo. I hope it challenges you, as much as it seduces you – kissing you full on the lips, while punching you square in the gut.

Above all, I hope that it heals you in the places that you can't touch yourself.

Holly Daffurn

www.hollydaffurn.com

Holly is also a director at The Word Association, a collective of writers from different backgrounds who are passionate about using their art form to make a social impact, offering poetry workshops and publishing opportunities to individuals suffering from long term mental health conditions.

www.the-word-association.com

CROSSING THE LINE

HOLLY DAFFURN

Dear Charlie,
I hope you love this book.
Thank you for your support.
Holly x.

BITE POETRY PRESS

First published in the United Kingdom in 2019.

First published in the United Kingdom in 2019
by Bite Poetry Press.

www.bitepress.co.uk

ISBN 978-1-913218-27-0

First Edition

Cover photography and design by Gerard Hughes
www.gerardhughes.co.uk

Printed and bound in the UK by Biddles, Castle House East Winch Road, King's Lynn PE32 1SF

For Paul, my Dad, for raising me on words and chasing away the monsters.

For Leo, my son, who questions, challenges and fills me with more love and pride than I ever believed possible.

For Gez, my partner in everything, for being my greatest source of adventure as well as my safe space. For believing in me, and believing in us… and for all of the beautiful things that we continue to make together.

CONTENTS

BRIDGING THE STRAIT

For Russia With Love

Red is your land
Like your bloody hands
As another body falls on the street
Red are the sands
Of time as they land
In each perfectly uniform heap
Each last grain
Must look just the same
Nothing challenging
Nothing too deep
Dear Russia, I grieve
For the lovers and love bereaved
Now they are reduced
To red meat

Sex is a matter of lock and key
But it's the souls that need to fit
Not the biology
Girls don't do girls like they're boys
Damon didn't know
How girls do girls like they're girls
When the lust starts to show

Krasni means red
As krasni means beauty
And red spells blood
And bloodshed is duty
And blood spilt is ok
It isn't a crime
When the blood spilt is gay blood
Police turn a blind eye

If you're painting a rainbow
You start with the red

But your country stopped there
Turned to dark clouds instead

Red was your voice
Was your blood
Was your choice
Was your flag-waving swell of sweet pride
Red was your birth
Your army
Your worth
Mother Russia... turn... to your bride

If I teach my son that love is love
That I don't have gay friends
I have friends who are in love
That I don't have straight friends
I have friends who are in love
And friends who don't need
Another human being to define them
Because being one whole person is enough
If I tell my son that love is love
And the Disney ideal of boy meets girl
They fall in love within five minutes
And get married without exploring each other
Sexually
Spiritually
Emotionally
Is an unhealthy reflection of reality
If I tell my son that love is love
And in love there is no gender
In Russia
He'd be taken from me
And put into care
Which seems so damn uncaring

You call it propaganda
When we talk about love
You've made it illegal
The powers above
You're breeding hate crimes
With your myopic views
Milonov, you're not far off...
That time...
With The Jews

Corrective rape
It's all red meat
Beat 'em 'til they break
It's all red meat
Gay girls in the ICU
It's all red meat
Bruised and abused
It's all red meat

Corrective rape?
It's the shape of the state
Motherfucking Russia
Let go of the hate
You call it a
"Disorder of sexual preference"
And we're not allowed to even drive
But the disorder in your heart
Means you're barely alive

"IT'S THE **SOULS**

THAT NEED TO **FIT**

NOT THE **BIOLOGY**"

Pulse

I hope you dance with your eyes shut
I hope you dance with your eyes shut
and your heart cranked wide open
or better still...
your eyes huge and hungry
only seeing that one target across the room
who throws you a smile so bright
that it burns straight through into your future
and at this stage
you can't say whether it will be just for tonight
or forever
but his look is so loaded
that is makes you heart stutter
in rapid fire
as your pulse quickens
and I hope you dance with your eyes shut

I hope the music was so loud
that you didn't hear *his* entrance
that you were flying in a place where pain can't quite reach
that you fell with a grace that felt like a continuation of
your dance
that you fell with a grace
that you learnt from a lifetime of
fighting your corner in love
and I hope that you dance with your eyes shut

I always felt safe in a space
where it's ok for your friends to wear their sexuality with a
rakish tilt
without fear of violence
I always felt safe in a space
where people tell you that you're beautiful
even if they don't want to fuck you

I always felt safe in a space where I could click with a chick
without it being seen as a treat of a show for a lecherous
male audience
because when girls kiss
your hard on is the last thing on their minds

Can we hear the word Orlando and think of the world
sculpted by Virginia Woolf's poetic novel?
Can we think of a world where sexuality
is not seen as a choice?

Think of the ditzy glair of Disney if you must
think of fucking oranges
but never forgetting that they are not the only fruit
when suppressing your sexuality is as easy as
suppressing oxygen
we are choking on the wrong words

So I hope you danced with your eyes shut
burning like a meteor
when you 49 bright souls fell
through the darkness
you left behind you an arch

In memory of those who lost their lives in the shootings in
The Pulse nightclub, Orlando, Florida
on the 12th June 2016

So Your Wife

So your wife hates my lips
She reads fellatio
Pictures the swell of your dick
She can't lip read, she doesn't know the truth
I put my lips to a much better use
Weaving words to inspire, encourage, delight
To chase out the shadows that haunt you at night
It's words that I give you
A different relief
Yet, she's searching for semen
In the glint of my teeth

So your wife hates my hands
The caress of a masseuse
Is all she understands
She's no musician, she doesn't know the truth
It's my fingertips that get the most use
That these thick pads, calloused and raw
Show devotion to the instrument
That makes my heart soar
That my nimble fingers and strong hands
Please you as an artist
And not as a man

So your wife hates my pins
She reads seduction
In my barely keeping it in
She can't see, she doesn't know the truth
The way I dress is mania put to good use
My lack of boundaries, my style liberated
Simply means I haven't been medicated
Matching mental disorders, a different connection
I see understanding
She sees attraction

So your wife hates that I'm bi
She sees girl-on-girl as a treat just for guys
She's never fucked a woman
She doesn't know the truth
That I've liked girls since Quatro stirred up my youth
It's not a sexual kink or a sign my morals are loose
And no, I'm not greedy, I don't pick and choose
I'm aware of my sexuality
Does that really make me a threat?
Perhaps she just hasn't met the right woman yet...

So your wife hates my youth
I'm not even that young
But I'm younger than you
And she's even longer in the tooth
She can't see, she doesn't know the truth
That my life experience has been put to good use
I've lived enough life for six
It's wisdom I offer, not perky tits
It's insight I give you, and intellect
She sees firm curves
and marriages wrecked

So... I hate your wife
She's taken you from you
And withdrawn you from my life
She can't see, she doesn't know the truth
That I only ever wanted
What was best for you
You see a person with depth, light and shade
She sees a slut who's out to get laid
She doesn't see
That the biggest threat of all
Is I've got you by the soul
And not just by the balls

MARK MAKING

Artists With Dirty Fingers

I like my artists filthy
restless fingers ink-drenched
the arid kiss of terracotta crumb
like your hands are the landscape
where your soul settles

Every still life is a dialogue
in my mind
I don't observe beauty
I articulate it

I love that you reel-off-your-machine-gun-fire-fury-of-
worded-bullets-with-such-sharpness-and-grace-when-
the-spotlight-forms-a-halo-above-you
but your mouth
searches for all the right words
in your snatched
conversations

I like my artists filthy
stories that spew with horrific emotion
reality and the grotesque decay of life
come to me paint-smeared
your fingertips dense with use
rosin-dusted trousers

Tap your fingertips to mundanity
let every tabletop be your masterpiece
as you seek out the soundtrack
that feeds your life

I like my art blood-streaked and raw
the roaring in the vocal
the chisel cruel enough to cut bone

Your world is framed and shot
captured
as you pervert the rule of thirds
into exquisite fractals

Just weaving to the bar to buy a second coffee
is a dance to you
your tip toe trip graceful
against the endless grey of the floor
Your fingers nibbled by needles
your mind a canvas of chaos and colour

Crowds become orchestral
you draw out crescendo
with each grandiose gesture

I like my artists oblivious of audience
world-absorbed
self-unaware
when the line between the canvas
and the hand
does not exist

The thrill as you reveal each
new piece
of art
and all I can see
is you

“SHE’S GOT WHIPLASH

CURVES

LIKE AN AMPERSAND

BUT TIGHTER”

Mistress

You look to me expectantly
Miss Immorality
And ask who I'm seeing
I say I've got a mistress
You can smell her on my fingers
She wraps round my tongue
Like deft linguistics
She's a soul igniter
A keep me up all-nighter
Got whiplash curves like an ampersand
But tighter
I'll pull over in the car
Just to hear her voice
Push into her soft spots
To hear her rejoice
Lost in her form, her rhythm, her pace
You see... my little mistress hasn't got a face
It's words that seduce me
Words are my life
I'm not playing away
I'm in the place where I write

Blank Canvas

Next week is a blank canvas
I want to thread it with your eyelashes
the collision where our smiles meet
the smudge of your fingerprints
warm it with your breath
and push the imprint of your story
into each fibre
soak it in your sex and substance
capture the tears
and the delicious rip of your laughter
I want it streaked with every colour of you
yet my gallery is crammed with portraits
that I recognise with shut eyes
there is no room for new
that doesn't stop me
picturing you

Intimacy

You say you didn't make a move
Though you surely cast a line
And the line was formed of heartfelt words
And words are fractured rhymes
And rhymes are where my heart resides
As language forms my blood
So although you didn't make a move
You touched me where you shouldn't have
For to touch someone with your words
Is the most intimate of acts
Once you lick someone with your language
There is no turning back

"ONCE YOU **LICK**

SOMEONE
WITH YOUR
LANGUAGE

THERE IS NO

**TURNING
BACK"**

HEMISPHERIC

The poems in this section were commissioned by Apples & Snakes in 2015 as part of their Home Cooking series. The full collection of recorded poems was called 'Both Sides of the Sky' and is available to listen to online.

Both Sides

You strip back my eyelids
an invasion of blinding brilliance
the morning-after
filled with bloody realisation
your laughter is the clatter of empty bottles
thick as the stash of phone numbers
the only rejection you've ever known
is an exhausted bank card

you are my fly too close to the sun
wing-singeing beauty
my excess
my abundance
the lavish in the gift
dripped with jewelled generosity
such loud
blinding splendour
that makes eyes and nations fall

you are
the loudest voice in the room
and the shortest skirt
you are
bite off more than you can chew
but swallow it down regardless
boundaries obliterate
the concept of personal space
does not apply to you
except in reference to
the entire galaxy that rages within

your mind is like central station
a tapestry of colour and opportunity
set to an insistent backdrop

you shoot for the stars
but fly far beyond

you are
the yes before the question mark
faster than the speed of life
retina burning
in your brilliance

sleep is for mortals
you brush it off with impatient fingers

you sign me up for everything
that terrifies me
then leave without a word

flicking the switch
as you shoot out the door
casting my world into darkness

where your sister grips me
clammy with neediness
stripping me of your finery
she is
the slow descent into grief
when no-one has died
she is
the terror in the morning light
she plucks my self-belief from me
and crumbles it to ash
she has never known a day without rain
she kisses my throat
and the swelling burns to the spleen
she pins me to the bed

with her bone, cold limbs
and persistent cracked kisses
her tongue laps against
the tide of my regret
her insistence
a blade that seduces me
her laughter
the death rattle in the box of pills
she is
the steel on steel
that stole my brother
she is
the darkest shade of emptiness

you both
exist in separate realms
slamming against the membrane that divides
never beside
you have a shared tendency to visit
without invitation
your luggage ominous and hazardous
as it clutters the hallway of my mind
I have lost track of all the ways in which I've failed
to evict you
my unwelcome house guests
I've stopped wondering where you go
when you're not with me
I've started learning who I am without you

Cut

My blood day
I am moist with menses
Womb full as the moon
We buy knives without question
Weighty steel
Sharp enough to cut bone
and the fleshy stratas above
The glint of the blade
entices
even now
But I will not act
I just need to lean against
The safety of its weight

Grief

When you died
People literally crossed the street
To avoid me
Walking the cliché with nervous feet
Like death is contagious
And killing yourself
Is somehow more terminal

At the funeral
Everybody told me I was beautiful
As though pain
Had altered my features favourably
Or vanity
Is a girl's mother tongue

Look after your parents
They urged
I was a child
I could barely look after myself

They didn't mention you
Or how you lost your head
Sorry for your loss
They'd mutter
Words as downcast as their eyes
As if we'd mislaid you
Through carelessness
Which is precisely
What we did

Birthright

In my blood
your stories curl like smoke
Each jolt of an ending
the fickle spark of conception
fixed in the double-helix
The burning welt of tragedy
shackled to sorrow
and the bleak reminder of consequence
I didn't inherit your hands
just the dis-ease
that forces them
You plunged art into the heart of me
clinging to the blade of the sword with two edges
the flair of creativity
ignited by insanity
This is my birthright
my rich inheritance
The gnarled roots of the family tree
bitten and rotten by the shame of decay
The branches
touch the heavens
The bipolar
squirms through the biopolymers
Two shades of intensity
coil around each other
Seductive and serpentine

Dear Depression...

Dear Depression
you're welcome today
I feel you wordlessly slink in the back-door
clinging to the shadows
nibbling off the raw ragged edges
of remorse
I need you today
for right now
I am the one in the white coat
I want to circle you
with inquisitive eyes
find the heart of you
measure its skittish dance
I need to study the ebb and flow
of your darkness

Your fur is matted and dank
I'm not edging closer to draw out your softness
to make you sleek and appealing
I need the roughness of your tongue
and the squalor of your stench

Bring your worst to me
lay it at my feet
a putrid present
overripe organs
swell into bloody juices
let me lay it out
on the pristine, white board of my paper
the perfect cadaver
and dissect it
with the sharpness of this pen

"DISSECT IT

WITH THE
SHARPNESS

OF
THIS

PEN"

BORDER STATES

The Eyes Have it

So we're dropping bombs on Syria
a place we'll never go
like throwing hate at hatred
makes us bigger somehow
Do they think, if we keep the noise of war
roaring loud enough
it must just block out the sound
of children dying in the dust?
And we're wearing our submission
in the way that France likes it
on our knees for America
because we're too small to fight it
And our stories go back too far
to recall why we're friends to start with
And our stories go back too far
to even have a heartbeat

Some people would rather stay silent
in a boat that's slowly sinking
than rock it or rebuild it
or do some real heart thinking
And when all we're armed with
is our opinions and our mouths
it's time to take the higher powers
on for ourselves

Because dropping bombs to stop a war
is like stealing from someone to stop them being poor
or paying your lover to stop them from whoring
or blocking your ears to stop yourself ignoring
We can't hear the bombs drop
and we can't hear their cries
and we can't see the blood
when we're plugged into Murdoch's lies

And it's human nature to look away
and not catch the eye
of a great power almighty
of whatever god on high
And fear brought us religion
and religion brought us fear
and if it wasn't for religion
then we wouldn't be right here
They pervert divine words
into the worst things of all
when humanity starts to lose touch
the world starts to fall
You can justify "collateral damage"
you can call it what you like
but nothing can forgive
how playing god
preys on innocent life

“ARMED

WITH

OUR OPINIONS

AND OUR

MOUTHS”

Born

You were born on the kitchen table
spewed into life
on a tide of blood and shit
flooding against the mug rings
reminders of the desperate comfort of tea
your chubby limbs beating out against the glassy solidity
bitten by the pen knib
barely protected by the hymen of paper
virginal white
his last words
still traceable
her fingertips find them nightly
now she arches against the stability of the wood
and draws you to her
you so wide-eyed and alien
smeared with newness
she prays that you will be like your father
in all ways... but one
you were born on the kitchen table
where his fingerprints still linger

Womb To Rent

A girl's face is public property
with comments of
"You're looking tired" and "are you sleeping properly?"
or else it's
"Gosh, you're beautiful!"
when you're actually trying to speak
but your audience is distracted
by the way your eyelashes sweep
or the angle of your cheek

Your body when it's youthful
is something you should keep
museum style... untouchable
so everyone can peep
or even grasp
hot hands on arse
just guys upon the street
your Donald Trumps, the men you dumped
like every little curve and bump
stops you from thinking deep

And a girl's womb is public property
an open space... to rent
like you're awaiting installations... applications sent
you hit a certain age
when questions start to bubble
"Is it not time you had some more?"
"Is fertility causing trouble?"
"You got knocked up the first time,
are his not swimming right?"
or else they tilt their heads sideways
and glance down to waist height
scanning the globe of your belly
in search for signs of life

A girl's life is public property
as if we haven't got a choice
like your length of skirt and ways you hurt
obscure the fact you have a voice
and we all know that wearing makeup
actually lowers your IQ
and your choice of career
influences who wants to fuck you
when I say that I'm a writer
the reaction tends to be the same
but you're much too pretty for that
are you sure you have a brain?

A girl is public property
open access... free for all
everybody gets a slice of her
and front-row tickets to watch her fall
so let's stop treating girls like property
and accept what they're willing to share
you can grab, grasp, push 'til she's naked
but you still won't get her soul bare

This girl is not public property
you can grip me until I break
but it's when I choose to let you in
that your foundations will shake

Factories

In the packed food factories
they put labels on tins
But the labels don't always match
the food that lies within
It's conveyor belt convenience
but labels are not lenient
And carrots can only be carrots
no matter how many times
you call them peas

In the hospitals, the birthing suite
they put labels on the newborns
Before they have the chance
to stitch up what's been torn
It's conveyor belt convenience
but labels are not lenient
And a baby can't speak or detail
what it feels like to be female

In your childhood, your school days
they label all the students
Boys and girls in classrooms
toilets – ladies, gents
It's conveyor belt convenience
but labels aren't so lenient
And sometimes the body you're born into
doesn't match quite how you feel

They ask me if I sense a loss
or if I need to grieve
Do I feel like my daughter's
been snatched from me in my sleep?
Has my motherhood been compromised?
do I feel like I've failed?

Am I longing for the child
who I knew so long as female?
When you came to me
you said that you didn't understand
How you'd always been a girl
but you're growing into a man
And I couldn't be prouder
of how you took things in your hands
It's hard to build foundations
when you live on shifting sands
But you're breaking all the boundaries
you're the king of your own land

So conveyor belt convenience
and labels that aren't lenient
will never give you freedom
And I guess the key ingredient
is knowing how you're feeling
and having the strength to reveal it

Your courage is inspiring
and I'll never stop admiring
How your life story's transpiring
your mind is so enquiring...

You know more about yourself
than people twice your age
You've got a sense of purpose
that obliterates the beige
And conveyor belt convenience
can fuck right off and leave us

Because what you're making is pure art
and you've carved it from your heart

I'm sorry that the body I built you
isn't the body that you needed
But we're working on a place
where you'll finally get your freedom
We're building you with pronouns
a new name and a new style
And since you've been a boy
a new confidence and smile

It breaks my heart to know
that so many people are still trapped
They can't tell their loved ones
how their body's got them wracked
That they're stuck inside a place
that will never feel like home
And labels upon labels upon labels
have got them broken

If we keep on talking, working, acting
we can close the factories down
We can box up all the labels
and burn them to the ground
Because conveyor belt convenience
and labels that aren't lenient
Are damaging our children
and they're worth listening to

Because they understand that gender
is more than what you're taught
Identity is something
that grows and is not bought
'She' is a huge label
for a boy to have to bear
It's greater than your wardrobe

and the clothes you're forced to wear
It's louder than the name you're given
and the cut of your hair

The packed food factories
are losing all their power
They can't get the staff
the business has turned sour
With conveyor belt convenience
we've broken the glass ceiling
Now all the factory drones
are working from home
They're making what they want to
they're making it their own
And some is blue and some is pink
but one tone stays – screw what the others think
And conveyor belt convenience
and labels that aren't lenient
Got burnt in the rubble
when they tore the factories down

So the packed food factories
are putting labels on tins
But they're leaving them open
it's up to you what goes within
The labels are all blank
they're as clean as a fresh start
It's up to you to design them
to find the colour of your art
It's conveyor belt convenience
but labels can be freeing
If you use them
to tell the world
exactly who you are

THE 180° RULE

You Built Me A Castle

You built me a castle
and out of each window
an achingly British landscape
stretched wide as your generosity
in completely the wrong shade of green
And the staff that you placed
were silent
but the language that had carved each face
was distinctly
unfrench

You built me a castle
with roofs that reach and grasp
their slant mimicking the skyline
of the city
where we fell in love
a place built on decay
Under its magnificence
a necropolis
where cemeteries spill into civilisation
and tombstones gaggle like artists
in cafés
dancing fingers wrapped in the scent
of Gauloises
where egos clash as ash drops
and stories shape the city
more than buildings

Under our foundations
the dusty bones of this union
keep piling
in silence
You loved my spirit
as I loved your seriousness
and a 14 year age gap

feels intoxicating
until you exhaust the ways
to bridge the gulf

And you built me a castle
you fashioned spires, turrets and mouldings
as French as madeleines
et croquembouche, gâteau à la broche et mille-feuille
et construit avec la même élégance

But behind those heavy doors
(that weigh on my chest
like the worst shape of secret
the truth that you are too scared
to admit to yourself)
Behind those doors
in the heart of this castle
that you insist is mine
the staircase looms
a Jacobean monster
the stained glass is Victorian
and as graceless as the great queen's profile
and to reinforce this laboured Britishness
from the cold plains
stare the face of the men
who lived on words
as we dine in silence
Chaucer, Shakespeare, Spencer
in all their wisdom
have no answers for me

You built me a castle
that despite its vastness
could not fill the void in my heart
where Paris still raged

When I yearned for the darkness
of La Seine
it was in his eyes
that I found enough depth
to pour myself into
The place in my blood where
France & Ireland collide
constantly seeking out
a home in this impressive structure
and in him
I found a place where I could stay still
and stay myself

You built me a castle
but I left you there
I took our five children
and the new one
who we all know
belongs to you
like the Chateau Impney
belongs to the Loire
Her dark eyes tell of secrets
that even my bilingual mouth
cannot find the words for
I have taken them to a place
that feels more British
more humble
more sincere
We do not need spires
that puncture the sky
Even the sharpest architecture
cannot prick pinholes
in the grey canvas
of this land
You cannot inject culture

into a place
like a vaccine
This structure sits on the surface
of its surroundings
like oil
refusing to blend
shimmying fish-like
colours you can't grasp
like each tone of me
slipping through your fingers

You built me a castle
in the shape of my heritage
and to my tastes
but stone is cool to the touch
and scores of bedrooms are hard to fill
even with children's laughter
and the fluidity of the piano
our family joy gets lost in these high ceilings

You built me a castle
from your status and money and power
and no one can deny your generosity
or the thought behind it
You built me a castle
but I always imagined love to
look more like freedom
My dear Raven
you built me a castle
so breathtaking in its beauty
but what I really needed
was a home

(for Anna O'Meara whose homesickness inspired the building of the Chateau Impney)

Piss

You still piss with the door open
Like a tom cat
Marking territory
You still splash the word
Wife around
A word yellow in its stagnancy
You still wear your ring
A complete circle
Although every ripple of a vow
Has been broken
The stench of piss is hard to shift

Grip

You will never love me like I want you to
And when you say you're proud
The 'o' circles me like a snake
Until my ribs grip my lungs
You feed me apologies like poison
Measured doses
That build
With lethal slowness

"THE

'O'

CIRCLES ME
LIKE A
SNAKE"

Unbreakable

You've broken me darling
You've torn me to bits
Stripped the meat from me
In ravenous rips
You're coiled round me snakelike
I'm breathless, I'm reeling
You've shattered my heart
Pressed against our glass ceiling
I gave you my all
It's all that I had
You plucked it, you fucked it
In meat-greedy grabs
You left me with nothing
But anger and rage
And the fire in my belly
And these words on this page

You've broken me darling
Though it wasn't your intention
I let you abuse me
You thrived on the tension
Marionetting me softly
On your silk-spun self-doubt
Stretching my soft confidence
With your villainous clout

You have broken me darling
You've fractured our pairing
Torn the heart from us
I'm wounded and wary
I still love you darling
I love you the same
But I also love myself
And I don't love these games

So I'm leaving you darling
To find my own self
I'm leaving our carcass
And our crumbling house
But you're tied to me darling
I can't cut out the part
Because the place that connects us
Goes right through my heart
I despise you my darling
But I love what we made
So for her sake alone
I have chosen to stay

CROSSING THE LINE

My Life In Your Hands...

Your hands that gripped the maple neck
drew music from between the frets
that made me ponder what was next
in the song and our lives newly connected

Your hands that found the shape of mine
guitar calloused fingers soon entwined
and asked to stand the test of time
we exchanged rings to seal the line

Your hands pointed fingers
your hands kept order
your hands hemmed me in
with violent violet borders

Your hands that found me in the dark
your hands that left the darkest marks
that prised my life and thighs apart
left bruises like prison bars

Your hands that begged me not to stray
gripping tighter every day
that rubbed my light and soul away
eroded at my inner grey

Your hands are empty
your hands are bare
your hands search on
but I'm not there
you tell them that we just grew apart
but your hands know the truth
and so does my heart

Fairytales

You treated me like a true princess …
waiting until I slept
before touching my flesh
punishing my drunk nights
with the weight of your desire
while the stale morning chill
lit the backdrop of denial

And I slept like I was dead
I always sleep like I am dead
And he was in my heart
as he was in my head
and any other man would have kicked me out of bed
but you chose to sentence me there instead

It caused 100 years of slumber
Sleeping Beauty's bloodied prick
but I never spilt a drop of blood
at your persistent dick
Yet the bruises bloomed like roses
twisting, tangling free
a briary hedge between us
where the sunlight ceased to be

In the blue morning light
I'd stitch the wounds you caused in bed
scared in case that the emperor's clothes
used that self same thread
Your character was drawn as a good man
I was painted as the whore
so my truth came out as fairytales
from my seat upon the floor

So the years piled high and heavy
like an 100 mattress stack
until even your lightest touch
threatened to make me crack
You set out to prove my frailty
I was tender, I felt small
and in the cold morning light
the scales began to fall

Your true portrait in our bedroom
showed the monster in the dark
but the world saw a softer man
which reality failed to mask
And our bed framed your darkness
with neat corners of four
you insisted that I wanted it
and so you gave me more

And any other man would have kicked me out of bed
but you chose to sentence me there instead

So I kept my stony silence
learnt from my darkest past
like every story book princess
from her tower made of glass
Like the mermaid whose tongue fell dumb
when all South of the navel came undone
but every story has a pulse
and its own spark of life
and dark truths can't stay buried
or the host will surely die
the truth will mount a mighty stead
and split its way outside

Your incubus was more toxic
than the prince of fairytales
you didn't kiss me to wake me
or cause bad magic to fail
You didn't kiss at all in fact
but you probed and pushed and took
and the ending remained unwritten
in this fucked up twisted book

Yes I fell for another man
Yes we overstepped the line
And what we did was immoral
but what you did was a crime

And I slept like I was dead
I always sleep like I am dead
and any other man would have kicked me out of bed
but you chose
to sentence
me there
instead

Car Keys

On dark days
you grip your name
like other girls
hold their car keys
between tightening fingers
and they say that
lightning never strikes twice
but you keep on getting hit
and the seconds between
the thunder and the sky splitting light
are not getting further away

We say that you are so at ease in your body
and that you are so comfortable in your skin
and you want to tell us
that it is not your body
sometimes you are still 14
and the bed is no longer your own
and your body is no longer your own
and the night is no longer your own
but the memory is still yours

And sometimes you are 17
and the first man who ever said that he loved you
is wearing your blood like a wedding ring
and you are carrying so much fear
you think you've grown a whole new organ
just to house it
but at least this time
you started out conscious
you had the chance to fight back
but you weren't strong enough
you were never strong enough

And sometimes you're still 17
and sometimes you are 23
and you tell yourself
he didn't mean to touch you like that
and the fear returns
and you are too scared to push him away
in case he pushes back harder
and in your language you are still working on
the word for no
and you are grateful that it isn't quite rape this time

Sometimes you make a sport
of collecting people's hearts
as though hearing enough
declarations of love
will stop you snagging your happiness
on the rough edges
where you put yourself back together
and every "I love you"
throws a light
that makes you look completely unbroken
even just for a second

I'm sorry that I don't tell you that I love you enough
I'm sorry that I put you in places that scare you

On bright days
you rise like a fucking phoenix
and we slip through your fingers like ash

"THE 'O'

IS THEIR
CLENCHED FIST...

"...AND THE 'O'

IS EMPTY SYMPATHY"

No

I said no
And they didn't listen
And the 'n' is a u-turn
That starts at the bottom
And dares to rise
Before crashing straight back down

I said no
And they didn't listen
And every pebble pushing into my palm
Is the small, round 'o'
Full, hard, unmoving
Every 'o' bites the flesh
Where the imprint of rock bottom burns

I said no
And they didn't listen
And the 'n' is scrawled in capital
Jagged, raw, red
An angry lightning fork of burning pain
Where does it hurt?
In all of the places where I once thought I was beautiful

I said 'no'
And they didn't listen
And the 'o' is the pain in a perfect circle
That licks my eye socket

I said 'no'
And they didn't listen
And the 'o'
Is inflated to splitting point
By the breath of silence
Empty, weightless, powerless

I want to cut it off at the cord
And let it float to safety
To obscurity
To anywhere but here
But it is tethered to the core of me

And the 'n' is an anchor
That weighs as heavy
As the sum of them all

And the 'n' is their clenched fists
And the 'o' is holding onto the last shred of yourself
So tight
That no one can steal it

And the 'n' is the knowledge
That they'll take it regardless
And the 'n' is the realisation
That you have been suffocating yourself
In the process

And the 'o' is their clenched fist
And the fist forms a lump in my throat
Where my silence was born
And the fist is the stone
From which forgiveness blossoms

My father asked you to leave
His bravery is fashioned from love and kindness
He says that I am gracious
In truth, I am too tired to fight
And victim is too heavy a label to wear everyday
And every time I stitch myself back together
I feel like I am stitching my very self shut
And I have realised that I would rather
Exist in pieces

Anything can be a weapon
In the wrong hands
And you loved me with that weapon once

And the 'o' is a wedding ring
That grips too hard
And the 'o' is hands around throat
And the 'o' sits silently beside the 9
I should have dialled repeatedly
And the 'o' is the fear that stopped me

And the 'o' is the empty response
to every difficult sentence
and the 'o' is empty sympathy
and the regret that I let you
get away with it

You caged me like a wild bird
And told everyone the colour
Of my wings
But wouldn't let them look
And in turn
I gave you freedom

I said no
And they didn't listen
And the word is too small
Insignificant
Powerless

So I took the word no
And gave it the company
Of other words
Let them grow together

Fed them the sunlight
That you starved me of
Crafted them a home

I took the word no
And amplified it
Honed its truth with rhyme
Let the story breathe

I said no
And they didn't listen
So I took their enforced silence
And built a stage from it
And stood proud upon it
Now I say the word no
And it gets heard
I own it in my palm
Look at it
Isn't it beautiful?
And when the no gets stronger
The yes gets louder

Now I say the word no
And it gets heard
You are listening so hard
It brings heat to the places
Where I know I am beautiful
You are listening so hard
You can almost hear its heartbeat
I said no
And you
All
Listened

OUT OF BOUNDS

“MY HEART

IS AS

PLUMP

PROUD

AND

INFLATED

AS THE ‘O’

IN THE WORD LOVE”

Meeting

You were in the theatre foyer
All height
And stripes
Those eyes
And that calming easy grin
Where I yearned to press my thighs
And I kissed you like an artist
By both corners of that mouth
And on every trembling cell
I left an imprint of myself
You were the right side of your partner
I was the right side of my spouse
But on every trembling cell of you
I left an imprint of myself
Your look it made me liquid
Your look it made me yearn
Your look ignited sparks in me
Where the future longed to burn

Realisation

The call ends
The weight of your last word
Has tipped me
Over the precipice
Where I was so carefully straddling
This infatuation
As the phone moves from
Cheekbone to desk
I feel my heart drop
Skydiving to heady new plains
My heart is as plump, proud and inflated
As the 'o' in the word love
And in its buoyant fullness
I finally understand
Why they call it falling

Patience

Everyone knows it
Just your name in my mouth
Makes me smile
I wear my love for you
As completely as the colour of my eyes
And as alive with light
With you near
I carry a secret slickness
Longing for the day
When you taste

Polaris

I've shown you the worst of me
And you're not running yet
You make me want to stand still
And live without regret
You've healed me in places
That I can't touch myself
And driven me wild
With your chaste hands and mouth

And lately, we've been close enough to taste
I've shown you the darkness I hide behind my face
And lately, we've been close enough to touch
And lately
I've been
Too much

You showed me that part of me
Was heading for disaster
And you got me to pause
With your kindness and laughter
I owe you my everything
You saved me from myself
And I'm longing to love you
With my hot hands and mouth
And lately, I've shown you I'm carved from disgrace
You've seen all the darkness I hide behind my face
And lately, we've been close enough to touch
And lately
I've been
Too much

You make me want to be a better person
In the worst possible way
It's not so much straying
As staying
True to myself
If you want faithful
I have every faith in you
You want truth?
I'll be true
To you
But what about being true to myself?
Staying with him
Would be the greatest dishonesty of all

I want to be the light
In your grey days
The right
In all the wrong ways
The faith
In the heartbreak
I'm here and I see you clearly
And I know that you hear me
My darling
Isn't it time?

A Good Hard Think

I undress myself slowly
In a place that's safe from harm
And press myself against the thought of you
Until you're liquid in my palm

Boxed In

You told me to put
Red, hot, sexy Holly
Back in the box
I should have heard
That you thought I was sexy
But all I felt
Was the sharpness
Of right angles
And parallel lines
And the weight
Of lidded darkness

Worth

So we're oceans apart
And I'm raging with dark
And you couldn't fucking handle me anyway
You're too good for me
And I mean that in the truest sense
You have a purity
That I could snap
With one bite of my desire

Animal

If I'm going to stand before you
All naked and open and raw
I'd much rather you looked at my tits
And my eyes
Than my soul and my past and my flaws
Since we breathed life
Into the word love
It stretches in the void between us
Like a wild cat
All velvet pads
Proud whiskers
Retracted claws
I keep it distracted
By the glimmering quickness of my lust
With humour
We keep the lust moving
Louder than the love purrs

White

Your scent is in bed with me
It holds me tight as your love
As I nap in the afternoon
I breathe you in
My sheets are blank page white
Unwritten stories cry from the creases
Last night you didn't go home
Expressions of love cling to the fabric

Medal

You hold yourself like an apology
The curve of the shoulders
Collapse against the weight of every
Am I good enough?
A defeated question mark
The silhouette of self doubt
I have my own admission
I'm sorry that I fitted so neatly into the space you left
When you grew apart

You hold yourself like an apology
Offered on rounded shoulders
You have withdrawn yourself and your sexuality so far
That it has gone out
I wear mine like a medal
And it is his neck that I slip it upon

"THE **VOWELS**

ARE **FULL**

AND **LOUD**

AND IN **MY VOICE**"

Selvedge

For decades
Sex was punctuated by the male orgasm
You write lines on my body
Where the vowels
Are full and loud
And in my voice
Our stories
Will never be concluded
One spills into the next
They are always exquisitely lit

Don't smooth things over with her
Keep the edges raw and jagged
Let that life unravel on the snag
We can weave new memories
I will lick the wounds
I offer you my heat
The heartbeat has died on your history
And I am pulsing with new beginnings

Refugee

If dust is made of skin cells
You have settled in the gaps
In my floorboards
With the same comfort
That you rest in our silences
And although the kiss of brick and mortar
Offers stability
Only in your arms
Am I sheltered
From the beat of my own heartbreak
Even with this restless heart
I have yearned to set down roots
That burrow through the place
Where our souls entwine
Even with this wanderer's heart
I have yearned to set down roots
That reflect the colour of my heritage
And I don't know what to call you
But your name fills my mouth to completion
All I do know is that
Each fibre of my being
Has never felt so vibrant
Or so alive
Yet I have never felt so still
I have never felt so whole
I've never felt so me
Through you I have learnt that I am enough
Through you I have learnt that I am worth it
Through you I have learnt that
Only when the roots are deep enough
Will I have the strength to touch the sky
Through you I have learnt that
My past is just made of shadows
And if we keep this fire burning

I'll never be able to place them
I came to you like a stray
Looking for nourishment
A place to lay my head
I only ever intended to pass through
In you I found a way to build walls
To keep my dreams from dying
I found the colour I could finally live with
If dust is made of skin cells
Then I'd wait forever
To let you build beneath my feet